Success Dreaming

An Entrepreneur's Guide to Investing in a Success-Filled Business Experience

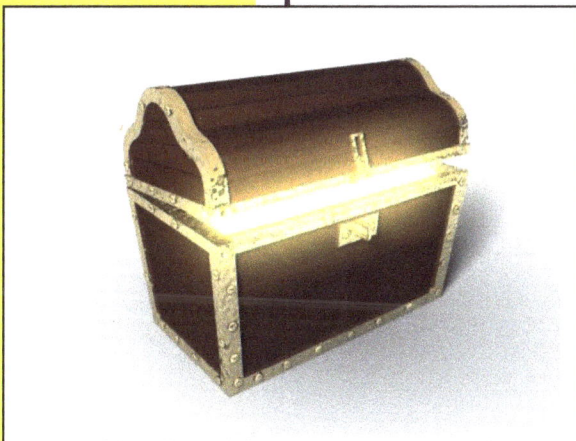

By
Laurie LaMantia

Table of Contents

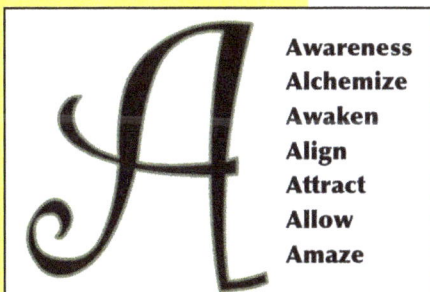

A
Awareness
Alchemize
Awaken
Align
Attract
Allow
Amaze

"To fulfill a dream…to be given a chance to create is the meat and potatoes of life. The money is the gravy." – Bette Davis

Success Dreaming

Welcome to this success experience! I wanted to give you a bit of background about how this workbook came into being. I created it for my entrepreneurship students as a part of the business planning process. I wanted them to imagine the business success they desired, even before they had a business idea. This workbook is a result of those classes. It is intended for entrepreneurs and would-be entrepreneurs to create a felt-sense of the business success you desire

At the opening ceremonies for Disney World of Florida, someone said to Michael Vance, who was Dean of Disney University and a co-creator of Disneyland, that it was a shame that Walt had not lived long enough to see the Florida amusement park's completion. Vance's quick reply was that Disney World existed only because Walt Disney (the man) could in fact see it from the moment he began to work on the idea. Mr. Disney could see in his mind's-eye almost every detail of the park as he formulated the plans for it. Long before the ground was broken for construction, Mr. Disney knew exactly how it would look and feel once completed.

This workbook will give you time to dream of a business experience that is fulfilling and prosperous, enjoyable and exciting. It is an opportunity to create your vision, your dream of what you would love to create and experience in your business life.

Look at this as an opportunity to:
- Consciously create what excites and interests you for your business life.
- Create free and clear of limitations and constraints.
- Pull to you the business experience that you really would like to have.
- Feel your power by intentionally directing your energy toward what you choose
- Move from wishing, hoping and wanting to attracting, choosing and embracing.
- Be in the driver's seat - taking the wheel of your car and going where you want to go.

Please give yourself permission to make the time to play with possibilities. Choose to proactively attract to you the business and success experience you want. I know through my many years of studying and teaching the law of attraction and the creating process, that success begets success. *Success is a state of being first, not the result of effort.* Focusing on success before, during and after, will create a successful experience the whole way along the journey.

So, as we embark on this success journey together, please keep in mind that to see in your mind-eye the successful result of your dream and focus on success – pure success.

Success Dreaming process is for anyone really and it is especially suited for entrepreneurs who want to create a successful business and the successful feeling of living life to the fullest.

Enjoy Success Dreaming!

Success is a state of being, not a result of effort.

TheAbundanceCenter.com

Introduction

Invest In Your Success Dream!

Most business planning processes begin by asking you to assess why you want to be an entrepreneur and if you are cut out to be an entrepreneur – then they have you jump right into business planning – outlining the marketing plan, operations plan, manufacturing plan and financial plan. You dive into the details of the business like how are you going to build and sell your product? How much is it going to cost? What are contingency plans, etc? All this is done before you do the most important step. There is a step - a vital step that comes between the "do I want to be an entrepreneur?" and the "thinking through the details of the business plan". This workbook is about that vital step of investing in the *energetic success* of your venture before you invest one dollar. This process helps you prepave the success of the business via investing quality and quantity of success energy into your dream business.

◆ *This is an investment process*. This process is more than visioning, creating a vision statement or a detailed plan - which have you in your head working through the business details but not necessarily the "vibe" of the business or your vibration as you endeavor in the creation of business. This process is an investment process where you are aligning your energy with the success you desire. How you vibrate as you create your business is what lays the groundwork of the successful business. So, if you are focused on success – you are investing in success. If you are focused on not failing – you are <u>not</u> aligned with the success you are seeking.

◆ *You are the power investor*. So really this is an investment book with you as the energy investor. Many entrepreneurs think they are creating the business plan so they can secure investors – the people with the money. But the entrepreneur is forgetting that he/she is the most important investor in the business. You are **the** primary investor, the energetic investor that paves the way for the money, success and anything else the business needs.

◆ *Align to success first – then act.* As a matter of practice, most of us believe that taking action is what we need to do. Get moving; "just do it" are admonishments to do something. I would like to interject the notion of aligning to success first, and then take action. This process will help you align to success first…by focusing on your success dream, learning what success feels like in your mind & body and creating a felt sense of success - this paves the way for successful action. The actions may be the same, but because the energy behind them is success, the actions will more effectively foster.

All things are first created in vibration.

©Laurie LaMantia

- *Give yourself permission to dream.* Envisioning the experience, the one you really want, the kind of company you want to create and be a part of, the life you want to lead while building it and living with it. This important step needs to be undertaken ideally before your head starts working on the details of the actual plan. Because many of us get so wrapped up in the details of the plan – we forget about why we got into the business in the first place or what we were really excited about creating. The outcome of this experience is that you will have a tangible powerful reminder of what you really wanted to create. Optimally, it is that blue sky, wouldn't it be great if statement, that is created from the place of possibility and wonderment.

- *Focus.* This process is similar to what Hugh Heffner did when he first contemplated Playboy. According to his True Hollywood Story he locked himself in a room for 3 days and wrote and wrote. He articulated what he envisioned he wanted to do, what he wanted to create. He said a couple of months later he was able to purchase the Playboy Mansion and he was off to the races…never looking back. This is a man who planted the seeds – powerfully, with intention and made his dream come to life. And you can to!

- *Write it down.* Writing gives us power and focus. Taking the time to write your responses into this workbook will help you get clear about what you are creating and will plant the seeds for your future success.

- *Be careful not to create a business as a reaction to the past.* When starting a new business, we might think we are creating something new, but really we are creating in reaction to the past. Like you did not like the way your old business handled opportunities, or you saw busienss being done a certain way and just agreed to it. But both of these are a reaction to the past and not necessarily creating from today – from what *you* want today. This is why we have the awareness and alchemizing steps in this process which uses the wisdom from the past and frees us to attract clearly for the future.

- *Come to peace with your past before you embark on a new venture.* In the Awareness & Alchmizing sections, we will mine the learnings from your past experiences. They are valuable – but we need to put them to rest prior to undertaking a new business. By investing your energy into success going forward versus trying to fix or undo a less-than-peaceful-past experience, you will eliminate lots of baggage & trouble before you start.

- *Plant the seeds of a fresh possibility.* In the Attracting, Allowing and Amazing sections, we will plant the seeds of success. So let yourself go for it! Excite yourself with your desires for yourself and your business. Let yourself feel free to say, this is what I want without the rules of the past or the expectations of others. What if you give yourself permission to have it your way!

- *Listen to your inner creator.* Throughout this process listen to your inner truth and wisdom – your

Success is happiness – anyway.

©Laurie LaMantia

CONSCIOUSLY INVEST IN YOUR SUCCESS

♦ *Protect your buzz*. You do not have to share your dream with anyone – not yet. Let this be your private investment strategy of mapping what you want to experience. As you work through this process, you will feel jazzed. Protect your buzz by not sharing it with buzz stompers – those well-meaning individuals who don't really know what you are up to and cannot get their brains around it.

♦ *Release old rules*. Release yourself from the unquestioned assumptions and "rules" of creating a business and let yourself create something that breaks the rules and feels exciting. The more it *feels good to you* – the more powerful it will be.

♦ *Feel Good*. Give yourself permission to create something that feels REALLY GOOD because the better it feels, the more excitement and enthusiasm you will be generating. And this is momentum – energy momentum! Enthusiasm creates tremendous business success momentum, tap into it and you are tapping into a wellspring of power and ability to glide this business into reality.

♦ *Create momentum*. Creating momentum is your opportunity and your challenge. Right now, your business is an object at rest, a notion or idea, and an object at rest tends to stay at rest until energy is applied in a certain direction. The purpose of this workbook is to help you invest your energy to create momentum in the direction you want the business to head – not in the direction you don't.

   And oddly enough, most entrepreneurs are heading in the wrong direction right from the start. We have all kinds of unquestioned assumptions and deep beliefs that hinder our progress or set us off into the weeds. Deep beliefs like "I don't have the right stuff to have a successful business", or "business is difficult and failure is probable", or "the deck is stacked against me." We think that with hard work we will overcome all of this and more. And I do agree – with hard work and tremendous effort you can overcome much and create momentum – but there is another way, a more grace-filled fun way that does not leave your health tattered and your relationships in shambles. This process will help you create powerful momentum in with less-hard-effort.

♦ *Lay the groundwork for success*. By working through this process – you will be laying the groundwork for a joy filled business experience that has been launched in a powerful direction; one that does not need tremendous effort to push it "onto the right track". As I said – enthusiasm, excitement and a powerful vision that feels good to your heart and soul goes a long way toward creating momentum and success – and isn't that what you really want.

♦ *Refer back often*. This guide will also come in handy when things don't feel so good as you go about creating your business. Time will pass and things will come and go and inevitably entrepreneurs find themselves questioning if they should be doing this and why do they feel so crappy about this venture. But you will have an important touchstone of help – your original vision articulated in these pages.

Remember: As you intentionally invest in working through this process you *are* taking powerful action toward bringing your success dream to life!

The Process

The process we will be working through is designed to help you focus your energy, to clarify your desires, and attract to you what you really want. It plants the seeds of future success through the following steps:

1. *Awareness* – We begin by reflecting on past experiences and agreements to use this data to inform your now choices. Becoming clear about what you are agreeing to with respect to owning and operating a business provides valuable insight.

2. *Alchemize* – Alchemizing is the process of turning lead (old experiences and feelings) into gold (new wisdom energy for the future). You will take the past agreements and transform them into new understanding and energy. Nothing will be lost, and the learnings of the past will be incorporated into the future. Alchemizing resistance from the past, frees up your energy for future investment.

3. *Awaken* – Here we begin with some fundamental belief structures that will greatly improve the results of your efforts. Awakening to your inherent creating power, understanding some of the mechanics of conscious creating and awakening to the wealth and success energy all around you, make this process happen effort-lessly and enjoyably.

4. *Align* – It is very effective to ready your mind and body for doing the best work possible. In this portion of the investment process, you are taking the valuable step of preparing your mind and body by raising your energy, clearing your internal and external world of clutter and moving into your heart.

5. *Attract* – Here, you magnetize your desires to you by *feelizing™* (*feeling* and *visualizing* as enthusiastically as you can) and consciously directing your thought, word and action energy toward your desired, dream business experience.

6. *Allow* –This "step" knows we have done the good work of planting the seeds of our desires into the fertile soil of possibility. Now you can flow in grace and ease toward your business experience. Allowing feels like rowing your boat gently down the stream, as people, ideas and all manner of help arrive to move you into your business experience.

7. *Amaze* – Here you notice how things are working out and you will be amazed at the help, guidance, and luck that seem to just be happening. This is amazing to notice. You will amaze yoruself and your will be amazed at how much fun you are having!

TheAbundanceCenter.com

How to Use this Workbook

This workbook is as much about understanding the process of conscious investing as it is about helping you to create the kind of success experience you desire. As such, it would be valuable to read through it once and get a feel for the overall process and then come back and create in it. There are three basic phases to this process:

1. Awareness of what your current and past beliefs/agreements are.
2. Awakening to an upgraded understanding of how the earth is set up to be your creating playground.
3. Attracting what you really want.

It will be helpful to do the awareness aspect of this process, then take a break and switch gears for a bit. The reason is that the energy for understanding the current reality is different than the energy of creating what you want and imagining what you will live. So read through the awarenss step, work through it, and then take a break – maybe even for a day.

Next, read through the awakening part of the workbook and incubate on that information for a bit. The awakening concepts are provided to help you shift into an energy of seeing how much love and support you is around always and in all ways to assist you in the creation of your success dream.

The next phase of this process is the attracting phase…where you use your imagination to bring your success dream to life. Here you will feelize your dream, making it a reality in your mind and body to the point it is not a matter of IF the dream will happen – but when. In this phase you will align your energy to the success you desire and artculate what you want to experience while feeling it in your body.

There are 7 "steps" broken into 3 phases if you will. Phase one is Awareness and Alchemizing, phase two is Awakening, phase three is Aligning, Attracting, Allowing and Amazing. The process is written sequentially to acknowledge the fact that the energy of the phases is different.

Note: If you do want to work through this whole workbook in one sitting,

- I would spend a few minuets preparing yourself for this work by takeing some deep breaths, shutting off your phone and maybe lighing a candle. Then set your intention to pave the way of your success.
- Next move to working through the Awareness and Alchmization steps. Take as long as you need to reflect on your current agreements and success beliefs…your agreements about how business success will happen. When you feel you have explored the past and current agreements, take a break and jump around to change your energy.
- Then come back and read through the Awakening step, allowing yourself to let the concepts seep in and raise yoru energy to the exitement of how much love and support there is for you.
- Then take a break and jump around in excitement for the next part…where you will use the truths of the awakinening step in combination with your imagination and success energy to Attract and feelize your success dream to life.

Awareness

Of Your Past

Alchemize

Your Agreements

Awaken

Your Power

Align

Your Energy

Attract

Your Dream

Allow

Your Desires

Amaze

Yourself

Chapter 1

Invest in Awareness:
Of Your Past

Mine the gold of your past experiences and learnings to:

♦ Understand your beliefs about being in business and creating a business.

♦ Understand your assumptions about success, failure and sacrifice.

♦ Understand inputs from well-meaning others (friends, parents, teachers, etc.).

♦ Get clear about what you want and don't want.

Awareness
Alchemize
Awaken
Align
Attract
Allow
Amaze

TheAbundanceCenter.com

"Business is in need of transformation. Our outmoded ways need to give rise to a new way...a way that integrates mind, body and soul back into what we do." - Anon

1

Understand Agreements

It is time to become aware of our unquestioned agreements.

The Awareness part of the Easy-Does-It process is really quite simple in that we are trying to become aware of any unquestioned assumptions we may have about our success. These are the conditions we have come to agree to that will impact our success going forward. The thing is that many of these conditions were created earlier in our lives, based on experiences we had or things we were taught. Therefore, they might not be that obvious to us, and thus why they are unquestioned or unconscious.

Some of the agreements we are taught early on are usually based in scarcity. If we saw our family struggle in a family business, we might have come to agree that it is a struggle to be in a family business. If we were taught that there is only so much to go around, we might believe in a limited amount of success (some get it and some don't). And success is usually based on conditionality, you need the right contacts, or the right education or you need to look a certain way.

This might sound a bit obtuse but *an unquestioned assumption that we hold shapes the energetic foundation of our business creation.* Why does a one person become successful and another with essentially equal qualifications not so much? Unquestioned assumptions - deeply held rules and beliefs that are either supporting our success or that are putting a lid on what is possible, because of what we have been told, or what we have seen, or what the world thinks (collective consciousness).

You are a powerful investor and you have the power to attract (create) anything you desire. You create by what you invest your attention in – through what you think, feel and believe – so it makes sense that if you have thoughts that are not in alignment with the success you desire, it is helpful to become aware of them and decide if you will choose to agree with them going forward. There are no right and wrong thoughts by the way…only thoughts and beliefs that will bring you closer to what you say you would like to experience.

The awareness part of this process asks you to reflect on your past experiences and *get clear* about what you think and have come to believe about success, being in business and doing business. This clarity provides a choice point – about what you will agree to going forward with respect to building this business dream. You might find you have many beliefs that support your success dream, awesome. And if you find some that are not so helpful, let's alchemize them and create something fresh and more aligned to what you really desire.

To be honest, I wish this awareness part of the process were not necessary. I wish we could have a desire and just imagine it into being – free and clear of old agreements (that are not helpful). But alas, for many of us, these old unconscious agreements shape our future success – whether we realize it or not – and they recreate experiences until we see them and choose anew.

Be kind as you do this.

Mine The Gold

It is time to mine the gold of our past learnings and agreements.

It is important not to reject the past, as it has provided you with *valuable information*: what you enjoy (and want more of) and what you don't (and don't want any more of). So you are going to look at your past and mine the gold of it. Looking at it as the gold mine it is - rich with learning and growth, full of information to create with.

Most people try to move forward with positive affirmations or a positive mental attitude but deep inside they have some *fundamental beliefs* that keep them stuck in past or current reality - recreating experiences they really don't want again.

This introspection work is so powerful because you will get clear about what you think and believe and then you are at choice about what you will hold onto going forward. It is similar to cleaning out your mental sock drawer. You pull everything out and look at it, then sort it into piles – keep, mend or recycle. Keep some beliefs because they work for you, mend some because they have merit they just need some updating, and recycle what is old and does not serve anymore.

The gold of our past is comprised of beliefs (assumptions) we agree to and are based on…
- ♦ What we have come to believe based on what happened "back then".
- ♦ What others have told us to believe that we assume is true.
- ♦ What has always been and we assume will continue to be so.
- ♦ What currently is because if it is then it must be true.
- ♦ What we saw others experience that we think is probably true for us too.

As we have discussed your dreams need your enthusiastic energy - free and clear. So look at the beliefs and assumptions you have accumulated and sort through them. Mend or recycle them to make sure you have a clean supportive mental slate that allows you to be aligned mind, body and spirit to your desired success dream experience.

You may want to read through the pages in this section and then let them roll around in your mind for a bit – so that insights can come. Ask yourself to become aware of any beliefs that are important to your success. Some beliefs are right at the top of your mind, but others need percolate to the surface. Then as they pop up write them down. You do not have to do this whole section in one sitting. In fact you might not be able to. That is ok; it is worth a bit of investment for the clarity.

Understand Beliefs

Beliefs about being in business…

What do I believe about being in business? What do I think about having my own business - really? What are my beliefs and assumptions around business and making money? Around business and freedom? Around business and relationships? Just rattle them off, don't think just write as many down as you can…

"What you have done is unimportant compared to what you are about to do. How you have erred is insignificant compared to what you are about to create." – Neale Walsh

Understand Beliefs

Beliefs about what you are going to have to do to be successful…

What do I believe it will take to be successful? What am I going to have to do? If I were honest, I would say I am up against… Who has to agree to it? What do I need to let go of to have it? Do I need to "give something up" or sacrifice something? What concerns do I have about creating this business?

Understand Assumptions

Use your past experiences to inform your future.

♦ Negative thing(s) I learned from past jobs...(I don't want to experience again.)

I will mind the gold of learning. Now, I choose to restate these negatives into fuel for moving forward. I choose to have these new experiences...

♦ Positive things I learned that I want to bring forward with me...

"Nothing can stop the man with the right mental attitude from achieving his goal. Nothing on earth can help the man with the wrong mental attitude." – Thomas Jefferson

Understand Assumptions

Worries, doubts or assumptions about your ability to be successful.

"Classic" Assumptions that limit ...

- I don't have the right_____
- I don't have enough _____
- (education, money, experience, support, motivation, help, capability, time, talent, creativity, connections,)
- I don't know the right people.
- I am not in the right social club
- I am not ready
- To be honest, I know things like this don't happen to people like me.

Understand Inputs

What have I learned from others?

What I saw/learned as a kid (from my family and parents) about business and being in business?

What do my friends believe or say?

What does the world say?

What other inputs have I seen and heard? From grandparents, teachers, siblings, etc.

What does God say? What does my religion say?

Self-actualizers are free from reliance on external authorities or the good opinion of other people. – Maslow

CONSCIOUSLY INVEST IN SUCCESS

Get Clear!

Know what you don't want to get clear about what you do...	
What I Don't Want	What I Do

Capture the things you don't want to experience or have happen on the left side...then flip them over and make affirmative statements of what you do want.

9

CONSCIOUSLY INVEST IN SUCCESS

Aha!

What am I realizing?

Now that you have a bit of clarity, (Go back and read though all of the notes and writings you have done.) What are you noticing? What conclusions might you draw? Be gentle and compassionate with yourself...be willing to see something you have not seen, or have an AHA. This might be the first time you are seeing and feeling and what you really believe. Spend a moment in silence, recognizing where you might be getting in your own way. Capture it here...

CONSCIOUSLY INVESTING IN YOUR SUCCESS

Ready to Let Go!

These are the agreements or experiences I am ready to let go of and transform into something greater:

1.

2.

3.

The one I really want to let go of is:

These agreements and beliefs are what we have invested in to this point in life – do you want to keep investing in these going

1

Chapter 2

Invest in Alchemizing:
Your Agreements

♦ Transform the lead of your past learnings and experiences into golden new energy.
♦ Release resistance
♦ Don't spend too much time – see it, alchemize it, move on.

Awareness
Alchemize
Awaken
Align
Attract
Allow
Amaze

Problems cannot be solved by thinking within the framework in which the problems were created." – Albert Einstein

Alchemize!

It is time to alchemize the old to make space for the new.

The next step in the Easy-Does-It investment process is Alchemy. It is a process of taking the old beliefs and experiences and transforming them into new energy. Alchemy is the ancient process of turning lead into gold. We are taking the lead-based old thoughts and transforming them into the gold of new energy and fresh possibilities.

For many of us the old lead-based beliefs act like resistance, as they do not really feel good or support our success dream and our intentions to experience it. For example, one of the old lead-based beliefs that you might be transforming is the belief that success is conditional, and that you must fulfill some prescribed equation of brains, talent, education, hard-work and lineage in order for you to experience success.. Now, take a moment and feel into this belief that *"success is conditional."* How does that really feel to you? If you are like me it is frustrating or angering. *How do I get this magical combination and how do I ensure it will work - for me?* Frustration, anger, confusion, hopelessness are all forms of resistance (as they do not feel good, and can act like a energy road block to the success you would prefer.)

So let's alchemize our old agreement(s)

Remember – Easy-Does-It

Take the old agreement that you really wanted to transform from the awareness section....

The Alchemizing Process

The Alchemizing Process:
1. Acknowledge the old agreement/issue
2. Allow it – as it is
3. Become Peaceful with It
4. Thank It
5. Replace It by Reaching for Something Greater

- **Step 1 – Acknowledge It** -The first step is to **acknowledge** the belief (or issue) and how it makes you feel. See it as it is - without judgment - just say hello to it. Bring to the forefront the agreement or issue that feels like it is standing between us and our business desires. Feel it before trying to move away from it. Don't pretend it does not matter, nor try to skip onto something greater or different before honoring the issue.

- **Step 2. Allow It** - To be **allowing** means to not fight against what showing up right now and being present to how you feel in this moment. Try not to reject the feeling or throw it back, walk away or get angry at it or yourself, or jump into fixing it prematurely. These are all just forms of resistance (energy invested into the thing we don't want to experience any more.) Right now, just notice the feelings that rise as we think of the belief that has come up for alchemizing.

- **Step 3. Become peaceful with it** This step is quite beautiful in that we can now see how this was part of our journey which brought us here. We are on the path toward conscious business investing and this is a very powerful and exciting path to be on. Somehow this issue served us and we experienced it for a reason. We came to believe and act the way we did for a good reason. It helped us survive and get through life.
    - If you had a tough boss who made your life miserable, it is helpful to see that and transform the energy from anger and resentment to peace by talking yourself through it. *"I am glad I finally saw what was happening. I see what a difficult situation it was. I am now going to use what I learned for my future betterment. I am thankful I had that experience and this opportunity."*

- **Step 4. Thank it** – for what it has as given you and taught you. Thank it for showing you the contrast to what you *really* want. It was there for a reason and you are thankful for the new understanding and growth it has brought. To be grateful for something is to stop resisting it, to see it and acknowledge it, even if the gift is not immediately apparent. As you thank it for helping you, protecting you and giving you what you needed, you are alchemizing it from something that was a problem to a friend with a gift.

- **Step 5. Replace it by reaching for something greater.** Now is the time to reach for your highest thoughts when it comes to this business. Reach for something greater...invest in the ideas that are fresh and new.

Transform!

Have An Alchemizing Ceremony

For some of us, having a tangible short ceremony to signify the intention of transforming this old belief into new available energy can be valuable. So, you might want to have an alchemizing ceremony. Set aside 15 minutes or so, not much more and intend to transform the energy of the old agreement by visualizing this short process.

- Begin by breathing to a count of 4 or 5. Just breathe in and count to 4 or 5 and then breathe out and count backwards fro 5 to 1. Do this for a few moments and allow yourself to get comfortable and relaxed.

- Next, imagine taking an old belief like...*wealth is conditional* and putting it into a "golden sack" that is sitting in your navel center. Fill the sack with all of the energy of the issue and all of its emotional energies. Feel the old hurts, worries, emotions and issues being gathered in the sack. Feel the anger, frustration and hopelessness gather into the sack. Let all of it be gently and effortlessly accumulated in the sack at your navel center. Feel the tension release from your shoulders and back. You might even be carrying the belief around in your lower back or hips. Allow yourself to release the energy into the bag. Allow yourself to be free.

- *"I put this into the golden sack along with the sadness and frustration, the worry and doubts of past. I allow myself to transmute these old energy feelings. I allow myself to release all the old investments and let them go.*

- When the bag is full, pull the golden cord closed. Surround it with your love. Bless it, thank it, and be at peace with it. Then see the bag surrounded by a white fire that is transmuting the whole thing - bag and all its contents. Feel the energy being transformed back into new potential. Let the old energies go from you heart, or hips, or head, or wherever you have felt it lodged.

- Breathe deeply and say, *"I transform this old energy, releasing it, I am at peace."* Sit for a bit, as the white fire is lit and engulfs the bag. Gently transmuting the energy. Spend a moment thanking it then lovingly releasing the past investments and agreements, making the energy available for fresh new possibilities.

- Do this until you feel the energy has completely been alchemized back into fresh energy and the bag is completely disintegrated. Breathe and feel the lightness in your body. Feel clear and free. Sit for a moment and enjoy the clarity, freedom and excitement.

- Now gently reach for something greater – you might have something that pops in your mind or just feel that you are now allowing your wealth in...simple and effortlessly.

- You may want to stay in this place of repose and relief for as long as feels good.

5

Reach for Something Greater!

It is time to reach for your highest thoughts and greatest desires – choose what you will experience now with this refreshed energy!

DREAM ELEVATOR STATEMENT

Fill in the blanks.

I have always wanted to…(what you would love to create)_____

I will do this by…(what the business gives/shares)_____

Unlike…(past experiences)_____

I will feel…(what you will feel)_____

And in 5 years…(the future possibility for the business)_____

For Example:
I have always wanted to…create a way for people to know their power
I will do this by…creating books, CDs and workshops.
Unlike… when I was in corporate
I will feel… free, enthusiastic and prosperous
And in 5 years… I will be free of financial fears forever

Chapter 3

Invest in Awakening:
Your Power

- Open to new possibilities
- The Law of Attraction is always in action
- You are an amazing Creator
- The tools for creating are within you and always have been.
- You can wire your brain for success
- Create from within and let your inner wisdom create your outer reality.
- Invest Wisely
- It's OK to want what you want
- Know that what you want, wants you!

Note: This chapter is about awakening to looking at you and your business in a very different way…

Awareness
Alchemize
Awaken
Align
Attract
Allow
Amaze

TheAbundanceCenter.com

Open!

Open to some new possibilities!

Before we move into attracting your success dream, it is valuable to **awaken to some new powerful ideas.** Awakening is the important step in any conscious investing work because we need to remember Who We Really Are (a soul having a human experience) and as such, the creative power we posess. So many people go through life feeling buffetted about, not realizing by investing their energy in a conscious way, they can have a much different experience. *By deciding how you want to feel in your business and what you want to experience, you are investing large amounts of energy that will magnatize the experience to you.*

Throughout this process, it will be very helpful if you hold and embrace these powerful ideas:

- You are a powerful creator, with the ability to attract to what you focus on.

- The world is your glorious playground – created for you to experience what you consistently vibrate as.

- Life is a smorgasbord with all possibilities already on the table – all you have to do is decide what you wish to partake of by feeling it. Investing your energy into success activates the law of attraction. Draw the experience to you by putting your attention on what you want (success) not on what you don't (worry about not having success).

- There is nothing you have to do to "earn" your desires, all you have to "do" is invest your enthusiastic attention energy on your desired business and enjoy the feelings of its success, even before the physical proof of it is here.

- There is no judgment about what you are creating – nor is there some Cosmic Santa deciding if you will get what you want or not because you were naughty or nice.

- The law of attraction acts like a Xerox machine – exactly reproducing your vibration – impartially and impersonally. So vibe (feel and think) how great it is to be in the middle of your wonderful business experience – now.

- Open to the possibility that what you really desire, desires you. And that how you feel matters more than what you do. Feel good, enjoy your days and watch how life shows up to support you.

- You live in an abundant and prospering world. Abundance and prosperity is the way of life!

You are the creator of your life. You are at the helm of your ship, take the rudder and sail it into whatever business experience you desire.

The Law of Attraction!

The Law of Attraction is Always in Action

Awaken to the power of the Law of Attraction. The Law of Attraction is like the Law of Gravity, it is in effect always, whether you are conscious of it or not. And it is your most powerful tool for creating the business experience you really want.

- o Attracting energy is magnetizing energy and you magnetize experiences to you through how you invest your attention, energy and focus on (e.g. what you choose to think about, speak about, believe about, feel and emote about.)
- o What you think about and dwell on happens whether you want it to or not.
- o How you feel (or vibrate) is an indicator of what you are attracting.
    - ▪ Feel prosperous, attract prosperity
    - ▪ Feel peaceful, attract peace
    - ▪ Vibe success, attract success.

- The essence of attracting is feeling. Feel what you would *love* to see happen. You are an investor investing your energy. So let the passion flow and give yourself an opportunity to really express what would make you proud to create and be a part of. What would make you feel "jazzed" to experience. The more strongly you feel about it, the more emotion (energy in motion) that is generated and felt, the more attractive power you are directing. This is powerful. There is an amplification of energy – momentum if you will, that creates a vortex that pulls your intention to you.

- If your energy falls – take a break, listen to inspiring music - and by all means get excited about what you are creating. Don't get too heady. Keep your judgments at bay. Just let yourself become absorbed in what you are attracting.

- Attracting is intending, believing, feeling, speaking, thinking, emoting, writing, doing - then repeating *until it is yours*!

- What you believe and feel to be true – becomes true for you.

- Like attracts like. Powerful attracts powerful, fearful attracts fearful, joyful attracts joyful, resentful attracts resentful…simple.

TheAbundanceCenter.com

"It is only with the heart that one can see rightly, what is essential is invisible to the eye." – Antoine de Saint-Exupery

CONSCIOUSLY CREATING YOUR BUSINESS

Create!

You are an amazing creator!

Awaken to the truth that you are a magnificent creator – born glorious and exceptional. This awareness is at the heart of this of this work. If you can give yourself the gift of knowing that, you will give yourself the ultimate power tool: yourself.

- *Understand your energy system.* Creating is understanding, directing and using your energy to attract your desires. The more aware and attuned you are to how you feel – which is your energy system attracting more of the same - the more you will be able to use your energy effectively to create. Life shows up the way you think, feel and say it will.

- *Use excitement and growth energy as a motivator.* Most of us have been taught how difficult business is. Statistics abound about how many businesses fail. This is a fear motivator, a way to get you to realize you need to prepare yourself for success. Yes, fear is a motivator, but excitement and possibilities of creating something amazing is also a motivator, a powerful motivator.

- *Create by Feelizing success.* Put your attention on what works, not on what doesn't. Put your attention on examples of success not failure. Daily, see yourself experiencing the business experience you would love to have. Feel it and visualize it – *feelize* it! And if you can't fully see it – then feel it, what does success *feel* like to you. If you are not sure, find out. Expore, ask, read watch, learn, listen and add to your defintion of success.

- The joy of conscious creating via energy investing give you the ability and excitement to realize your power.

- *Remember: Energy going into old habits, old beliefs, old thought patterns, and old approaches means you are re-creating more old experiences and there is less energy for your new creation.*

-

TheAbundanceCenter.com

Reality is what you create it to be.

CONSCIOUSLY INVEST IN SUCCESS

Use Your Tools!

The tools for conscious investing in your experience are *within you* and always have been.

Awaken to your investing tools that have been with you always:

- <u>*Your investment choices*</u> – Where and what you decide to invest your attention. Notice what you choose to say, think and do with respect to this dream business and its success.

- <u>*Your thoughts*</u> – What you choose to think about. Thoughts are actions, in that they are the genesis of experience. Pay attention to where your mind wonders when it comes to this business experience. Do your thoughts migrate to "can do" or "no can do"?

- <u>*Your beliefs*</u> – What you choose to believe about this happening. Beliefs are the thoughts behind the thoughts, the things we have come to agree to as true. And we tend to hold strongly to our beliefs. Explore what you really believe and assume about experiencing your dream and the likelihood of your success.

- <u>*Your words*</u> – What you choose to say (thoughts expressed). Your words have power. So, notice how you talk about this with friends and family. (So be conscious about who you talk with about it. You might be surprised what you end up saying. Just notice.

- <u>*Your actions*</u> – What you choose to do (thoughts acted upon). What do you spend most of your time doing with respect to this business plan & experience? And how *do you feel as you are doing it*?

- <u>*Your attention*</u> – What you choose to focus on and where you put your attention energy. Put your attention on what you choose – not what you don't. When you catch your mind wandering to doubt, worry, or fear of not experiencing this, gently bring it back to the excitement of your success dream.

- <u>*Your feelings*</u> – How you choose to feel or vibrate. You can choose your feelings. Get excited and passionate about the dream you are creating. Vibrate as success.

- <u>*Your heart*</u> – Where you choose to come from. Increase the probabilities of joy, peace and abundance by creating from your heart. *A huge secret is to create when you feel happy and joyful.* So spend a few moments getting into a joyful state of being, then take action.

TheAbundanceCenter.com

CONSCIOUSLY INVEST IN SUCCESS

Wire For Success!

You can wire your brain for success!

Awaken to the notion that you are already success*. If you are working through this book, you are probably at a time in your life when you are ready for something new…and that is tremendous! Yahoo for you!

- Many of us were raised in the "school of hard knocks" where life is difficult and there is a fixed pie of money, success and resources. The book *Think and Grow Rich* by Napoleon Hill is a book dedicated to helping people to wire their brains for success. Many of us were taught "poor" mental models, but there are a select few individuals who have been telling us for years that there is another way, the way of the "rich", the way of Carnegie and DaVinci. And is it time to embrace this new reality of life and your experience of what it can be. Start seeing the possibilities and the many ways in which life is sharing and supporting you and your success.

- I encourage you to try a new school, the "school of-knock-your-socks-off", where you start to realize that all of life was created for you to feel and know your magnificence; where the energy of life is well-being, prosperity, and power and is available to you always. All of life is constantly sharing and supporting you, conspiring to help you out. This new school of knock-your-socks-off says that the whole life process is meant to be an experience of constant joy, continuous creation, never ending expansion and total fulfillment in each now moment! How 'bout that for supporting your success!

- *Your opportunity now is to decide what you are going to agree to*. Your opportunity now is to start wiring your brain to see and feel success, to notice a support system that has always been available, and you have the power to engage. Your opportunity to is think like Carnegie and create like DaVinci!

  And because the Law of Attraction is always in action:
  think success, feel success, believe in your success and soon,
  the neural pathways in your brain will be hardwired for success!

Imagine a new reality, fresh possbilitites
and don't give in to the old agreements.
Create a new way – your way of success.

Create From Within!

Let your inner wisdom create your outer reality.

Awaken to the understanding that all things that happen in your outside world, originally were created in your inside world. There is a great difference between reacting to the outside world and how it operates versus living from your internal urges and wisdom. There is no end to the outside world's ideas of how things work and what we "should" be doing. The news, books, pundits, parents, even friends tell us what they think we *should* do, what can and cannot happen, the *rules* of success, etc. But this is letting the outside decide what is best for us. We are reacting to their opinion. When creating our success dream, we might react…

- Based on pain we experienced in past jobs (I don't want any more of that)
- Based on what others think business is and should be. (my mom says)
- Based on the past (this is how I saw it done)
- Based on what we see and read in the papers and books (how it is done now by others).
- Based on what Wall Street and other "experts" say (they are experts, they must know).
- Based on what we saw happen to family and friends (if it happened to them it could happen to me).

But these are a reactions to outer observation and not necessarily creating what you desire from within!

What we are up to here is creating your dream from your unique vision. It will be unique and uncharted because it is coming from inside you. Create by listening to your inner truth and desires. Yes, mine the gold of past experiences and let those inform your future choices. Learn from others. *Then*, listen to your internal urges, value how you feel, act on what you would like to experience - free and clear of outside dictates.

LIVE FROM THE INSIDE OUT.
LEAD FROM THE INSIDE OUT!
CREATE FROM THE INSIDE OUT!

Invest Wisely!

Invest your enthusiastic energy into yourself and your dream.

Awaken to the fact that you are a power investor. *Understand you have the power to make valuable and important investments (the most important investments): where to focus your energy.* Your business needs your energy, your positive, enthusiastic energy to get it going and to build momentum. *Invest* your enthusiastic life energy into your business!

Many people think they need money to invest in their dreams and hat money is the reason we cannot do the things we dream we want to do. We say, "When I have money *then* I will _____." And so, because we don't have the money, we let our dreams lay in the back of our life closet, waiting. But money is not the investment needed. We need to invest our energy into our success dream. *Money is not nearly as important an investment as quality energy focused on what you want to experience*; vibrating as the success experience happening now!

Investing Energy like…

- Attention energy –Feeling good and excited every time you think of your success dreams.
- Love energy – letting your heart marinate in the joy of your dream.
- Enthusiasm energy – the excitement and yahoo! energy that says won't it be great when my dream becomes physical! and "oh boy" I can't wait, and wow this is a great dream!
- Priority energy – making your dream an important part of your day – scheduling time for it first before the urgent other things use up your energy. Having conscious investing sessions when you feel good and want to invest well.
- Belief Energy – knowing that your dream is happening. Knowing that even though you cannot see it all yet, it is coming together. 99% of the work is done energetically – before you actually see the results in physical form.

**Even if you don't have the money,
you have something even more valuable to invest:
your powerful enthusiastic success energy!**

TheAbundanceCenter.com

"Only one who sees the invisible can do the impossible." - Frank Gaines

Know!

**It's ok to want what you want.
Know what you desire desires you!**

Awaken to the fact that what you desire desires you. Many people are afraid to desire or want things for many reasons from they don't want to be disappointed to they don't feel worthy of what they desire. Or they have been taught that to want is not ok and maybe even a bit weak. But desire is where dreams are born, and imagination put to good use. If you did not desire, you could not create, or wouldn't bother!

- *Desire puts energy into play.* Part of the mechanics of desire is that as you desire energy is created and focused on that desire, immediately - the energy of the thing that you desire is put into play. But it is in energy form - not physicalized yet. It is in sort of an energy bank account – a fulfillment escrow - so to speak. And when you are ready to experience it, put your attention, energy and focus on it, and it will start to move from not-seen-with-the-eye energy to physical "I can see it" form.

- *Get excited by your "fulfillment escrow".* This energy bank account was created by you, for you and is waiting for you. That is life working with you to help you out and that is the Law of Attraction on your side and in your corner. Life has your back and is working on your behalf to have you experience your hearts desires. If you desire it – life desires it for you! Why wouldn't it?!

    It is like the lovers – who find each other after a long time apart and they run into each other's arms. Imagine what it would be like to see something you have longed for and run toward it - *and* to see it running toward you! *Feel this attraction between you and your dream.* Your dream is the "hot" other you pine for that is pining for you!

    Your opportunity now is for you to decide what you are going to agree to. Your opportunity now to see and feel it is ok to desire and know that what you desire, desires you! You can notice the creation support system that you have the power to engage through how you invest your energy. Are you going to be a cosmic powerhouse or a measly human? And you are going agree that creating this vision is going to be difficult effort or a joyous opportunity?

Don't sabotage yourself with old notions of what was, support yourself with new notions of what can be.

Chapter 4

Invest in Aligning:
Your Energy

♦ The Power of ROA (return on alignment)
♦ Ready yourself by becoming present
♦ Raise your vibration and get happy
♦ Get excited to create your dream
♦ Spend time in appreciation
♦ Align with the energies of success, harmoney, prosperity, and all-is-well.

Awareness
Alchemize
Awaken
Align
Attract
Allow
Amaze

Ready Yourself!

Readying yourself by aligning to success is an important step in consciously investing in your dream experience. As we have spoken of, giving yourself the time and space to create what you want is vital. And the more empowered, excited and feeling good you are, the more you are planting seeds for experiences that will be a vibrational match to that.

♦ *Be a vibrational match*. We are preparing your mind and body to be in the most receptive empowered place to plant the seeds of what you want to experience. Try not to create when you are exhausted, frustrated or disempowered as it slows the process way down. If you are tired, it is not the time to do this important work, because you want to plant seeds for future success. You don't want to taint the seeds with tired energy; you want to plant the seeds with energy that is aligned to the vibrational energy you want to experience...success. Remember good energy in, good energy out - abundant joy in, abundant joy out.

♦ *Put an appointment in your day-timer*. It is helpful to be in the present moment and not distracted, so turn off the phone, and set aside *quality* time, maybe in the morning when you are fresh and have a good hour without time pressures to do this energy investing work.

♦ *Prepare your physical space*. It is helpful to create a sacred "space" that is conducive and symbolic of your intention to create and invest wisely. There are many ways to create a sacred space but the essence is sacred. Sacred, set apart or devoted to, the intent to create. You can create sacredness by lighting a candle, burning the same incense, sitting on the same cushion, and playing loving music. It is really up to you, but the key is to create a symbolic habit that tells your subconscious and your conscious mind that you are here to create.

♦ *Get happy*. First get happy, and then create. First you get happy, and then you create. So do the things that make you feel good. It could be going for a run, petting your dog, singing in the shower, Disco, whatever it is that will raise your vibration and energy.

The Law of Attraction is impartial. It will not judge if what you desire is inappropriate. Nor will it assess if your vibration is accurate or not. It just attracts a vibrational match to you. So, align your energy to success, fulfillment and knowing it is a done deal and let the law of attraction do its work.

Align Your Energy!

Aligning your energy means to become a vibrational "match" to that which you want to attract. If you want to feel good in this dream business, it is advisable to feel good as you create it. I cannot stress the power of getting aligned into an empowered, successful vibration – and then creating.

It is not about efforting, it is about aligning. So many people waste valuable time and energy because they jump into "doing something", taking action, before *doing* THE most important thing first: getting themselves into a higher vibrational place like success, joy, excitement, then taking action. This little shift from doing, to aligning then doing – will change your success rate dramatically…because the law of attraction is always in action!

Can you feel the difference between when you "feel good" (not just from a health stand-point) and when you feel not so good? When we feel good, we feel empowered, strong, vital, and vibrant! When we don't feel so good, we feel low energy, drained, tired, and lackluster.

Think of the song "what a Wonderful World" by Louis Armstrong, this song is aligned with love. He sees people shaking hands, saying how do you do, they're really saying I love you! Alignment.

Think of words like limitless, prospering, unconditional, free, abundant, success, glorious – or pick some of the ones that make you feel great. This is what we are going for. Feel great – then create! Feeling great – creates more feeling great! Isn't this what you really want anyway!

Watch your thoughts, for they become words. Choose your words, for they become actions. Understand your actions, for they become habits. Study your habits, for they become your character. Develop your character, for it becomes your destiny.

Be Present!

Quiet your mind and come into the present moment

Before doing the business creating work, it is helpful to transition from the day-to-day goings on and become peaceful in the present moment. Some like to read from inspiring books, others listen to uplifting music, others like to work out or do yoga to relax the physical body and quiet the mind. Do what you have found to work for you, to prepare yourself for this creative work and are able to focus and not feel distracted; to raise your vibration to eagerness for success!

☀

Investment Tool…Deep Breathing

Intention…to come into the present moment

This yoga breathing technique called Kumbhaka can quickly bring you into the present moment.

1. Start by bringing your attention to your breath. Just focus on the "in-breath" and the "out-breath".

2. Slowly, breathe in as deeply as you feel comfortable to a count of 3, 5 or 7. Then exhale to a count of 3, 5 or 7. Take around 5 breaths this way.

3. Next inhale to a count of 3, 5 or 7 and hold your breath in for a count of 3 or 5. Then exhale to a count of 3, 5 or 7 and hold your breath out for a count of 3 or 5. Don't strain yourself.

4. Really feel the core of your body expand while your breath is being held in and then feel the core of your body contract as you hold your breath out.

5. Do this for 5 – 10 in and out breaths and you will be very present.

(Note: people with heart conditions need to consult a physician before doing this tool)

CONSCIOUSLY INVESTING IN YOUR SUCCESS

Be Joyful!

Move into your heart and become joyful and excited by creating

The next part of aligning our energy is to move into our hearts. This essentially means coming to a place in your body and mind that feels good, where, you feel happy and joyful and empowered, while feeling that you are doing important valuable work to bring your business desire to you. When we create from our hearts, we create from a place of grace and from there no matter what we create, it will be for the highest, and holiest good of all. Again, you might want to read inspiring poetry or a book, or listen to music that opens your heart to a place of joy, love, unity and peace. Dance, sing, play air guitar, have fun and get excited to be creating!

✸

Investment Tool…Star Burst Method

Intention: to move your energy and awareness into your heart center

1. Begin by focusing your attention to the center of your chest just below your neck, and see and feel a brilliant star burst there.

2. Breathe in and out from the center of your chest, feeling energy swirling in and out of your heart with every breath, and extending all around and past your body.

3. Now see little bits of light, little iron particles of yourself floating around you.

4. Feel these glittery particles being attracted to your chest. You are pulling back the pieces of yourself that you have put into worries, fears, concerns, old issues and grudges…pull your energy back into your heart.

5. Feel light and energy flowing from all around you to your chest, as the starburst grows larger, stronger and more brilliant.

6. Spend a few moments here, feeling and expanding, becoming more peaceful, loving, and calm.

Appreciate!

Spend a few moments in appreciating

Take a few moments in appreciation for what is in your life right now and for the opportunity to invest in success.

Right now, I appreciate ...

One definition of appreciate is to increase the value of. That which we appreciate we grow, appreciation appreciates.

1

Chapter 5

Invest in Attracting:
Your Dream Business

- Describe your Dream - Ideally!
- Imagine!
- Feelize!
- Play with Possibilities!
- I want it because!
- Use what Works!
- Passion!
- Success!
- Now's Good!
- Share with a trusted friend!

A
Awareness
Alchemize
Awaken
Align
Attract
Allow
Amaze

Don't meditate ON your dream, meditate AS your dream!

Attract Your Dream!

Attract! Overview

It's time attract the business experience you really want!

The third step in consciously creating your dream business experience is to feel it, live it, and vibrate it in you AS you! It is to really play with feeling what you would love to experience. While you are doing this you might want to keep happy music playing in the background and give yourself permission to let loose and be wild. There are no right or wrong answers, let right be what feels good to you.

In the attract step, feel free to open to possibilities and feelize it. (Create a felt sense of you in your business experiencing it just the way you want your business.) It is like you are the author of a play called "I can't believe how lucky I am to be in this business" and you are scripting it just the way you want. Don't put anything in that does not make you say "ooooo" and "aahh". Don't put anything or anyone in that does not feel just perfect.

◆ *Feelize it!. Feelizing* is visualizing and feeling together - seeing your creation in your mind as well as feeling and getting excited about it in your body (like jumping for joy) by it happening in your life. You engage your creative mind when you visualize and see your business experience happening. You engage your body when you emote and feel your business as it is really up and running. Go to your dream business experience - feel it, see it, enjoy it, like it is happening right now. Focus your attention on the end result. Don't worry about the details of making it happen. Let yourself dream and vibe it into reality. Like enjoying waking up every morning and seeing *"You have cash"* emails from Paypal or getting a phone call from an unexpected new client who wants you to create a program just for them. Yahoo! Is your mantra.

◆ *Become it* – This business experience is already in the infinite field of possibilities – you are choosing it by living it in your imagination, in your minds eye, in your body. Become a vibrational match to your dream. This is how we attract it, knowing it is not a matter of "if" it will happen; it is only a matter of "when". Make "when" now, by being the success you seek right here, right now.

◆ *Don't get bogged down in getting it right.* Or worrying that it is not perfect. It is so much more fun to be free and play with this than try to get it right. When you catch yourself putting too much pressure on to make it just so you are stopping the flow of joy energy. Take a moment, take a few breaths and say, I am just playing with possibilities here. And go back to "wouldn't it be just great if…" and let your heart sing new options.

◆ *Let your nature take over*. A rose does not struggle to bloom; a bird does not struggle to fly. It is not your nature to struggle. Allow yourself to connect with your hearts desires and know it is part of your nature to move there. It is our judging mind, which jumps in and analyzes, and thus creates struggle. It is your nature to move effortlessly (read enthusiastically without resistance) to prosperity, well-being and fulfillment. Great fullness is your birth-gift! Enjoy it and allow yourself to connect to it.

Attract! Overview

It's time attract the business experience you really want!

- *Dream it to attract it.* The wonderful part of dreaming is you are in free space, blue-sky mode. It is from blue-sky mode, the place of unlimited possibilities where you heart is engaged and leading the charge. When you heart is engaged, meaning you are open to possibilities of freshness, you are engaging the creative energies of life to attract to you want you really want. Because as we spoke of, like attracts like, attract your dream, by spending time and energy in the fresh possibilities dream mode.

- *Write it out.* Writing or journaling your responses to the questions are very powerful, because it helps you focus and be in the present moment. So even though it is helpful to think about these questions it is even more effective to write your responses (notice you are not writing your answers because there is no right or wrong) write your responses from the place of "oooohhhh I can't want to experience this! Yahoo for me!"

- *Blue Sky it - Create free and clear.* One of the most powerful and freeing things to do for us is to create from a clean slate. In this experience let yourself imagine what is possible without the constraints of what you consider "reality". Most of us limit ourselves right from the get go with the limits of what we expect or have experienced. We place instant boundaries on the infinite…but not with this tool. This is your chance to create from the deep blue sky, where anything is possible. Let you imagination go, play with possibilities and by all means don't waste your mental energy on worry, doubts or those killer phrases like "It can't happen." Right now you are giving yourself permission to create from a clean slate!

- *Focus on what you want.* Consciously apply your energy in the direction of what you want to experience, not what you don't. Don't talk about what you don't want or discuss old hurts with your friends. This is giving energy to what you don't want. Be mindful of what you are saying to yourself and your friends and your casual interactions. Sometimes we try to be humble and say "well who knows if this business will happen, or if I get financing, the banks aren't lending" BluCK! Don't go there. Be careful what you say, you are listening!

- *Get congruent.* How many times have you said one thing and done another? Or said one thing to someone and said something completely different to another? And the old favorite, talking positively in public, but deep down you feel freaked out. You can't fool the creative ethers. What you really feel deep down is what is true. And how you feel behind what you say is what you are really attracting. So get congruent. Start aligning how you feel with empowerment (and what you want) and then talk, think and act in congruence with that.

- *Believe in it.* What would you do if the world wanted what you have? What would you do? What if you knew people wanted what you had or what you wanted to share? Create from this energetic place!

Ideally!

Ideally, I really want to experience...

Ideally is such a great word. It allows us to play in optimism. In this space, write out everything you can think about your ideal business. *Feelize it,* visualize it see your creation in your mind as well as feeling and getting excited about it in your body. When you think about your dream experience what are you feeling, how are you acting, what are you doing – *Ideally*! Talk about your day-to-day reality. Who are you interacting with? What would *be so great and make you feel so good! (e.g. you feel like you just won the lotto!)*

Spend time everyday feelizing and being excited about this experience

you just articulated.

Anything, which is created in the outside world, comes from within us. We are the creators, the genesis of all things; as such, we have tremendous power and ability to make all things happen – this is true creativity.

Imagine!

Imagine, envision and feel the business you are creating...

Use your imagination to draw your desire to you. If you can imagine it you can create it. In my ideal business experience...

- I feel...

- I enjoy...

- I really want to...experience myself as...

- I am using these talents...

- I am experiencing prosperity and abundance like...

- My ideal day feels like...

Play with possibilities!

Play with possibilities…

Wouldn't it be great if is a wonderful sentence starter because it allows us to dream and wish free of limitations. Feel how you feel when you say "wouldn't it be great if" your heart lifts and you are given permission to imagine fresh possibilities and play with unexpected outcomes.

♦ Wouldn't it be great if this business grew into…

Because…

♦ Wouldn't it be great if our customers….

Because…

♦ Wouldn't it be great if I….

Because…

♦ Wouldn't it be great if we became known for…

Because…

When people go to work, they shouldn't have to leave their hearts at home" – Betty Bender

7

Play with possibilities…

♦ Wouldn't it be great if the business generated…

♦ Wouldn't it be great if the business felt and acted like…

♦ Wouldn't it be great if we created "corporate charisma" by…

"There are four basic desires: *Dharma* the desire to find purpose; *Artha* the desire to fund the purpose; *Kama* the desire for happiness and enjoyment; *Moksha* the desire for freedom and bliss from unity with the Divine."
— From the Book <u>The Four Desires</u> by Rod Stryker.

Because!

I would like to create my own business…

Give yourself permission to be honest about why you want to create this business experience. Whatever you say and feel is fine and it is valuable.

I want this successful business experience….

♦   I want it because _____

And I will feel_____

♦   I want it because _____

And I will feel_____

♦   I want it because _____

And I will feel_____

♦   I want it because _____

And I will feel_____

The only limits are those you impose upon yourself.
Limitations are self-chosen.

CONSCIOUSLY
INVEST IN
SUCCESS

Use What Works!

What works?

It is helpful to use what you have seen in the world that works to give you a roadmap and idea of what is possible and what others have created that works. So take a moment and capture inspirations from what you have seen that you want to bring into your future optimal experience.

♦ What I have seen work that I want to experience also...

♦ A role model I would like to emulate and what they do or have that I want to experience...

Because...

♦ An actual company I respect that I would like to emulate...

Because...

50

Passion!

What is your passion? What do you want to share?

When you hear about truly wealthy, successful people, you find that their motivation comes from excitement and internal personal passion. They have a fire in their belly about something that they want to contribute, something they want to experience. They are driven from an internal fire, a passion.

♦ I am very passionate about...

♦ I feel strongly that I can contribute...

♦ I want to help by...

CONSCIOUSLY INVEST IN SUCCESS

Success!

Now!

What can you do NOW?

Why wait? NOW IS GOOD! You can start now!

♦ How can you start to get excited right now?

♦ What about this dream excites you right now?

♦ If you could do one thing right now that feels good in support of this dream what would it be?

♦ If you could think one thing that feels good about your business what thought would you hold?

♦ If you were to talk about his with your best-most supportive friend what would you say to them?

♦ If you had every resource at your finger tips, if you had legions of people in your employ to make this happen – what would you do right now?

3

Statement of Intent

This is what I choose for…

_____

(Tentative company name)

I choose to build a great company that

◆

◆

◆

◆

TheAbundanceCenter.com

Create a collage or "picture" of the creation here

This is what it feels and looks like…

Attract & Feelize!

Attract!

This is my vision for Our Customers…

This is my vision for our people…

This is my vision for our suppliers…

*Create new supportive statements of what you choose now.
Review and Feelize these often.*

Attract!

This is my vision for Abundance…

This is my vision for the Company Culture…

This is my vision for Team Work…

Create new supportive statements of what you choose now.
Review and Feelize these often.

Attract!

This is my vision for communication & decision making…

This is my vision for customer service…

This is my vision for creativity & innovation…

Create new supportive statements of what you choose now.
Review and Feelize these often.

FUN!

This is my vision for fun, play and celebration…

This is my vision for growth & change…

This is my vision for encouragement & rewards…

Create new supportive statements of what you choose now.
Review and Feelize these often.

Attract!

What I choose to <u>believe</u> about my business now…

<u>Assumptions</u> about my success I will now make…

The <u>experience</u>(s) I choose to have now…

Create new supportive statements of what you choose now.
Review and Feelize these often.

Attract!

How I *will* <u>speak</u> of this business now...

<u>Thoughts</u> I *will* hold about this business now...

Three <u>actions</u> I will take to bring this to me now...

1.

2.

3.

Accomplishments

These are the TOP 3 Accomplishments in the First Year…

These are the TOP 3 Accomplishments in 5 Years …

These are the TOP 3 Accomplishments in 10 Years…

Create new supportive statements of what you choose now.
Review and Feelize these often.

Share with a trusted friend

It can be very valuable to share this dream with a buddy. Be careful to choose a buddy that really wants for your best and has constructive supportive comments for you. Ask your buddy to hold in their mind and heart that they wish for you to be wildly successful and prosperous. Also, you would like them to share supportive ideas for bringing the dream to fruition.

♦ What did you learn from your buddy? What ideas did they have?

> Don't let life discourage you – everyone who got where they are had to begin where they were. – Richard I. Evans

3

Chapter 6

Invest in Allowing:
Your Desires

- ♦ Flow to your business with grace and ease!
- ♦ Trust it is all happening!
- ♦ Stay open to possibilitites!
- ♦ Act on synchronicity!
- ♦ Trust your inner wisdom!
- ♦ Be willing to receive!
- ♦ Passion!
- ♦ Release attachement!
- ♦ Be welcoming!
- ♦ Recommit!
- ♦ Take Action!
- ♦ Play!
- ♦ Embrace!
- ♦ Notice what is working!
- ♦ Choose the game you are going to play!

A
Awareness
Alchemize
Awaken
Align
Attract
Allow
Amaze

Allow!

It's time to allow your business come into your reality.

In the final step of this process, you will be moving effortlessly toward your desired business creation. Allowing is the feeling that things are moving along as smooth as buttah - there is no resistance, fears, doubts or worries. Allowing is shifting your energy from one of pushing and difficult efforting to following synchronicity - acting on your internal urges, honoring unexpected coincidences, and paying attention to opportunities that present themselves. Allowing is the experience of things coming to you in grace and simple ease; where things that seem difficult become a magical smooth experience.

♦ You have done a great deal of energetic work to this point. You have clarified and attracted what you would like to experience energetically, you have feelized what you really want, and you have alchemized old beliefs and made that energy available for this business. You have done a great deal! Congratulations.

♦ Now is the time to know the business is in progress, it is on its way. Yes there are going to be things to "do" but realize you have already done much. Again, you have already done much. Allowing is knowing you have done much – the best work – from an energy perspective - proceed knowing this creation is making its way into physical form.

♦ The more you can allow (agree it is coming, expect success, know you have been heard and the energy is in the process of physicalizing, the more quickly your business will come into being.

Investment Tool – Flowing
Intention…to enjoy and know the feeling of flowing

A wonderful way to get into that "flowing feeling" is by imagining yourself soaring like an eagle above the clouds gliding effortlessly through the sky. This might sound odd, but if we want to flow, it is very helpful to feel flowy. If you want to dance, it is helpful to dance – no? Other ways to feel that flowing feeling is to drive your car down the expressway later at night when there is no traffic and just enjoy gliding along the highway. Others feel themselves skiing down a hill or roller-skating, or running freely, or swimming in warm water. Whatever method you use, give yourself permission to engage your mind and body in the experience of flowing.

TheAbundanceCenter.com

Flow!

Dance with Life!

Allowing means to:

- **Trust –** what you desire, desires you. It is already in the field of possibilities; you are now pulling it to you, attracting it lovingly into your reality.

- **Dance & Stay Open to Possibilities –** because you trust your business creation is on its way, you can let go of worry, fear, doubt and befuddlement. You are free to play with life and enjoy the "discovery process" of how it comes and when it comes. You can feel free to be open to unexpected help and unexpected outcomes, dancing in joy and effortlessness to your creation.

- **Act on Synchronicity –** be watchful and alert to options that come and you feel this could help or this could move you there. Work with comes into your life by acting on it and trying things that you might not have in the past thought would work. Things are not always as they seem and some things (which you might not expect) might yield results this time.

- **Trust your intuition and listen to your inner wisdom** - Your body will help you, listen to your gut instincts and honor them. If something feels "right or good" go with it, if something does not sit right or feel right or if it "smells bad" – stay away or find a new way.

- **Be willing to receive** - Open to life helping you out, get ok with receiving as much as giving, pull down some of your barriers (whatever they may be) to let yourself open, accept and enjoy the things you say you desire and would love to have. This is a biggie! How many times we say we would love something – but push it away because we are not willing to agree we can have it (read worthy of it or earned it).

- **Release attachment and expectation –** T.S. Elliot wrote, "For us, there is only the trying. The rest is not our business." Creating is the opportunity to try, to give the experience our best effort. Allowing is releasing how it comes, and not worrying.

Play!

- **Be welcoming -** Make room for your business creation in your life and say yes to it happening. Be welcoming of all things that come your way. Do not judge what is happening. Trust that you are on your way. Things are not always as they seem and the things that seem to be not helping are most likely just the right things you need to get you where you are choosing to go. So release your expectations of how the creation needs to come and open to how it does show up.

- **Re-connect, reenergize, re-feel, recommit -** Spend time (say 5 minutes a day more if you can) reconnecting to the *joyful feeling* of enjoying your business dream. Get reenergized about it and re-feel what it is like when you are experiencing it. Feelize it again – visualize it and feel it a bit everyday. Don't worry about the details or making it happen, let your inner excitement pull the opportunities to you.

- **Take action and actively participate -** *Just do it*, don't let your mind talk you out of some inspiration because it seems silly or out of the realm of possibility. Nothing is impossible and anything can happen in the blink of an eye. So trust that little voice inside and go for it. You will have urges…call Sandy, schedule an appointment, make a reservation - act on them – *please*! Act as if you are in the middle of your creation happening.

- **Play! -** Play, play, play, with life! Creating is a joy and a marvelous experience…so play with possibilities, dance your creation into being, and enjoy watching your dream come to life. Celebrate how far you have come, give yourself a pat on the back. Don't let creating turn into a drag by getting over-invested in it "having to happen" or exchanging the playful, joyful feeling of inspiration, for the drudgery of doing. Remember play is the way…to creation realization. So, play…

CONSCIOUSLY CREATING YOUR DREAM

Embrace!

It's time *allow* yourself to have this!
***Embrace* it as a real possibility!**

This process is a process of creating change – a change for yourself to help you live in alignment with your dream and the things that bring you joy. But, when we are in transition, it is easy to feel discombobulated and off center. When we go through a change it is difficult to imagine that things are going to settle down and work. After having worked this far in the process – know you have laid the groundwork for this fresh new opportunity, for a change. It is now time to stop seeking and know you have found what you are looking for – embrace it.

You have imagined the most perfect situation you can muster, the ideal situation for yourself. *Allow* yourself to have it! *Embrace* it as a real possibility!

Embrace this dream as *your* reality.

When we embrace something we wrap our arms around it, we feel it and enjoy it. We hug it and give it our love. Embracing your dream, as a reality is one of the most profoundly powerful things you can do, because now your dream is getting your loving attention. No more seeking mode (a.k.a. "what if" and "maybe this" and "what about that?"). It is ok to still contemplate, but don't let this be your primary mode, or else you will always be in seeking mode and never "found" mode…don't hold your dream just out of reach just frustratingly far enough away that you wonder if you will ever experience it.

Embrace what you do know, now!

Embrace what you do find exciting and meaningful. You do not have to have the whole picture laid out perfectly to embrace the aspects of your dream you want. There is an unfoldment that is happening, giving you time to make modifications and enhancements to your dream. But that does not mean you have to hold the whole dream off until every "i" is dotted and every "t" crossed.

Take some action, now!

What action can you take right now, embracing enjoying this vision and taking one or two actions that feel like you are supporting and honoring this dream. No more and no less. Don't overwhelm yourself with it having to all be perfect. Take a step, then another, then another.

©2021—All rights reserved

68

Choose!

Choose the game you are going to play.

One of the things people often marvel at about entrepreneurs is they decide the game they want to play – and play it. They seem to be free thinkers and doers, and when they hold to their vision, they enjoy the game.

There is a wonderful analogy that fits here…and it is more how things really work. When you are playing a video game, you make choices and those choices lead you down certain paths in the game. You restart the game and different choices lead to different outcomes. And all of the choices you make and all of the outcomes are already in the computer game program. All the options are available; your opportunity is to choose.

What is being outlined in this workbook is very similar. You have just outlined your dream, and many of the specifics of it. You have invested powerful creative energy into its realization. You have just said "this is the game I want to play and now I am going to make choices to have this experience."

Don't try to fit yourself into other peoples' created realities. The most exciting part of being an entrepreneur and one of the reasons so many take this path is that they want to create their own reality. They don't want to live by another's rules and game that the other started playing. Entrepreneurs want to create their own game and this is totally terrific! And your opportunity as well! Create your own game, embrace it as if it is already there, and walk forward knowing even though you might not be able to "physically see it" yet, you can feel it and see it in your minds eye and success is assured. You can imagine it and daydream about it. And the more you give yourself the permission to agree to this new game that you are creating. The more you are allowing it to become part of your day-to-day experience.

Spend a few moments everyday, creating and feeling this new "game" and enjoy the success of it.

Conform and Be Dull. – J. Frank Doble

Chapter 7

Invest in Amazing:
Yourself

- ♦ Expect Success
- ♦ Amaze yourself by noticing successes
- ♦ Enjoy the Process

A
Awareness
Alchemize
Awaken
Align
Attract
Allow
Amaze

> Problems cannot be solved by thinking within the framework in which the problems were created." – Albert Einstein

Expect Success!

Don't meditate ON success – meditate AS success!

- The great Yogi, Pandit Rajmani Tigunait, advises his students to meditate AS what they are creating. _Become_ _what you are creating_. This is different than meditating on something – as from a distance. Can you feel the difference? One seems to be an idea, (mediating ON success) a nice notion for "someday", the other (meditating AS success) is an actualization of mind and body in real time.

- Ghandi said BE the change you seek in the world. This is Ghandi understanding the creating process. Don't pray for peace – BE Peace. Don't hope for change – BE Change! _Become_ what you desire in mind, body and spirit – then watch it materialize in the physical world.

- There is a great story in the book _The Isaiah Principle_ by Greg Brandon. Greg tells of how he and his friend David (an American Indian) were going to pray rain, as there was a drought in the area. David and Greg ventured out into the desert and found a sacred spot where David's ancestors said the "skin was thin between worlds" which the Indians had found as powerful place to create. David focused for a while and then said – "Ok, let's go." Greg said, "I thought we were going to pray _for_ rain!"

  David said, "No, we would never pray _for_ rain, that is like saying we agree to "the current reality of no rain." David said to "Pray rain" is to feel yourself in the middle of your new choice (experiencing rain). David said he feelized himself walking in the mud during the rain, enjoying the mud between his toes and feeling the rain on his face. He saw the crops growing and people trading those crops in the village. Then he gave thanks – not for the rain, but for the opportunity to choose a different experience. David _prayed rain_ by vibrating the reality of enjoying the rain. He did not come from a place of lack (there is no rain and we need some) he came from a place of enjoying the experience of rain. David was the change he sought in mind, and body.

Be the change you seek in the world! - Ghandi

1

Success Journal!

It is already happening!

Date	What I noticed today…(what surprised me, what was unexpected, what I thought was great, etc.)

Notice what is working - Everyday take a moment to notice what is working, the daily successes, the new ideas, the help, the unexpected support toward your business creation. Notice what comes along in support of your creative energies. This will help you log your progress. The Law of Attraction brings you more of what you put your attention, energy and focus on. Therefore, the more you notice what works, the more you will attract what works. It is so simple, and SO powerful.

Success Journal!

It is already happening!

Date	What I noticed today...(what surprised me, what was unexpected, what I thought was great, etc.)

Success Journal!

It is already happening!

Date	What I noticed today...(what surprised me, what was unexpected, what I thought was great, etc.)

Enjoy!

Enjoy and celebrate the business creating process.

What a joy it is to feel our creative power - what a wonderful opportunity to see and experience yourself in your full glory. The excitement comes in the learning and growth as much as in the attracting and having. Because each experience we have shares with us something - a piece of wisdom, an expansion in knowledge, an awareness of how dearly we are loved. Creating is just one of the exquisite ways we get to know and feel our true essence.

So notice what an amazing investor you are and notice how life supports and honors you. Enjoy the process of bringing what you choose into being. Choose joy and choose to enjoy the magical journey you are on. Notice that when you are enjoying and paying attention to how wonderful life feels and how magical an experience it is, how alive you become. You fill with awe and wonder; gratitude bubbles from within – just because – how lovely – what a blessing creating is.

Enjoy and celebrate what you bring to you.

"Life in the physical realm is glorious indeed and its purpose is to bring you happiness, through the awareness and the declaration, the expression and the fulfillment of Who You Really Are. Go therefore into this magnificent world of your creation and make of your lifetime an extraordinary statement and breathtaking experience of the most glorious ideas that you have ever had - of yourself." – God in *Conversations with God*

Chapter 8

Practice Re-Aligning With the "A" Process

REMEMBER TO:

♦ *Awaken* to what a powerful creator you are. Reawaken to your creating tools of energy investing, And remember wealth, success and support is around you always and in all ways.

♦ *Align* your energy and vibration to harmony, and success - feeling great, empowered and eager for your business success.

♦ *Attract* the dream business by Feelizing it – focusing on it, reliving it – as you bring it to life.

♦ As you become *Aware* of any thoughts or feelings that bring down your energy, *Alchemize* them by surrounding them with white light and letting the resistance of them go.

♦ *Allow* the success dream experience to flow.

♦ Be *Amazed* and notice how things are happening and know the momentum is building.

Awareness
Alchemize
Awaken
Align
Attract
Allow
Amaze

Practice!

CONSCIOUSLY
INVEST IN
SUCCESS

Practice Aligning your Vibration to the Success Experience you Want!

- The key to this process is *practice*…. doing it or some form of it. As you play with it and make it your own, you will find it becomes easier. Feel free to change it as you need to make it work for you. The key is the knowing you have the power to create and putting loving energy at what you choose to experience.

- As you work though this you may start to unearth all kinds of thoughts and beliefs you have come to agree to as to why you can't or shouldn't have the power to create or have your creations – Alchemize them! The more aware you become of these thoughts, the more you are at choice to decide if you will continue to agree with them going forward.

- You can apply the process by scheduling *Conscious-Investing sessions,* where you schedule time once or twice a week (more if you are able) to spend quality time focusing your energies in the direction of your creation – to attract it to you. Reread what you wrote, add to it. Some people do this by daydreaming, others through creative visualization…the point is to be clear and focused, loving and empowered - not leaving your creation to happenchance but making it an important priority in your life.

Anything, which is created in the outside world, comes from within us. We are the creators, the genesis of all things; as such, we have tremendous power and ability to make all things happen – this is true creativity.

Investment Tool:
Wanting, Happening, Done

This is a tool to help you move quickly from the vibration of wanting, to having - literally in a few seconds. It is moving from possibility to probability to certainty. The key is to practice shifting the energy in your body as you move through the steps. I will talk you through it here:

1. So when we want to have a successful business, we usually say, "*I want this to happen.*" The first energy we feel is usually wanting. Can you feel what *wanting feels like in* your body? It usually feels like, "I want this successful business...*but* it is not here" or "I want it...*therefore I don't have it.*" Basically, I want it and I am not experiencing it. It is important you feel the - *wanting and it not here yet* - aspect as the first step.

2. Next, you are going to tell yourself: *It is happening*! Feel the relief you have when you tell yourself the business experience you want is happening. It is in progress; your desire is on its way and you can relax a bit. You are moving your vibration from *wanting* the desire, to feeling the desire *happening*. Notice the change in your body; notice the feeling of relief as you let yourself feel it is happening and coming into being.

3. Finally, you are going to tell yourself it is *done*! Move from that feeling of *it happening* to it *being done*, a done deal! Yahoo! Now notice how you feel. If you let yourself agree it is done, you will now probably feel excitement, contentment, ease, peace, success, completion: all of the feelings of wanting something and then experiencing it come to fruition. That is the feeling we are looking for, knowing *it is done*. Spend time milking *this done* feeling as you can, because it is in this vibration you want to engage the law of attraction.

    Do you notice how you can change your vibration pretty quickly as you walk yourself through these three steps? You have just shifted yourself from the vibration of wanting (and not really feeling all that good), to it happening (which feels better), to it being done (and feeling even better).

    Play with this, as you go about creating your business plan. As you feel yourself "*want, but*". Invest in moving from wanting the desire, to it happening, and then to the feeling of it being done...and stay in the feeling of *done*. Get good at this, and you have the power tool of an energy investor.

TheAbundanceCenter.com

Quotes & Songs That Inspire Me

List Songs and quotes that are meaningful and inspirational to you…

Things To Remember

1. You are a magnificent creator – born glorious, exceptional and with the tools for creating naturally within you.

2. The world is your glorious playground – created for you to experience your creations.

3. Life is a smorgasbord, with all possibilities for you to experience already on the infinite table of life. All options are already in the field of possibilities – you are just attracting them to you.

4. You are worthy to experience your creation. There is nothing you have to do to *earn* your creations.

5. There is no judgment about what you are creating – nor is there some entity deciding if you can have it or not. There is only love and support for what you choose to create. (No judgment, assessment, rejection, etc.) Ask and it is given.

6. Like attracts like. What you put your attention on grows, what you take it from fades. Your thoughts, beliefs, feelings, assumptions, words and actions attract more of the same.

7. There is a creation process and creation technologies already in place that you use to create…deliberately or unconsciously.

8. Energy going into old habits, old mental patterns, etc recreates those experiences and feelings in the present.

9. Align then create. Align to the highest, best feeling vibration you can, before undertaking any project.

10. Attract by feelizing success. Attract what you want by BEing it versus thinking about it.

11. Alchemize worries, doubts and fears, by seeing them, thanking them, learning from them and then transforming them in love and peace.

12. Allow your desire to come to you in grace, ease and effortless enjoyment. What you desire, desires you.

TheAbundanceCenter.com

Resources

Books very helpful on this journey….

- Ask and It is Given – by Esther and Jerry Hicks
- Your Hearts Desire – by Sonia Choquette
- Manifest Your Destiny – by Wayne Dyer
- The Power of Intention - by Wayne Dyer
- Conversations with God, Book 1 – by Neale Donald Walsch
- Seven Spiritual Laws of Success – by Deepak Chopra
- The Law of Success – Using the power of spirit to create health, prosperity and happiness - by Paramahansa Yogananda
- The Holographic Universe – Michael Talbot
- The Isaiah Principle – Greg Brandon
- A Return to Love - Marianne Williamson
- The Art of Joyful Living - Swami Rama
- Think and grow rich – Napoleon Hill
- Rich Dad, Poor Dad – Robert Kiyosaki
- The Millionaire Mind
- The Secret
- What I learned before I sold to warren buffet - Helzburg

Movies that really show how this works…

- The Secret
- Under the Tuscan Sun
- What The Bleep Do We Know
- Spiderman
- Defending Your Life
- Forrest Gump

Songs that inspire…
- *Rocky Mountain High* - John Denver
- *I'm So Excited* - the Pointer Sisters
- *I can fly* – Usher
- *Just help yourself* – Tom Jones
- *With Arms Wide Open* – Creed
- *I hope you Dance* – Lee Ann Womack
- *I've Got The Power* – Snap

©Laurie LaMantia

Great Quotes

- "In order to keep energy coming to us, we have to keep the energy circulating. Like a river, money must keep flowing; otherwise it begins to stagnate, to clog, and to suffocate its own life force. Circulation keeps it alive and **vital**." – 7 Spiritual Laws of Success

- "What is the meaning of life? To find meaning in life!" – Michael Gelb

- "All flowers have an angel standing over them – saying "grow, grow!" – The Talmud

- "A fear is not a good enough reason not to do the things you desire to do!" – Sonia Choquette

- "Clearly I am not needed, yet I feel myself turning into something of inexplicable value. " – Mary Oliver from Buddha's Last Instruction Poem

- "You get what you think about, whether you want it or not." – Abraham

- Anything, which is created in the world, comes from within us. We are the creators, the genesis of all things; as such, we have tremendous power and ability to make all things happen – this is true creativity.

- "Play is often talked about as if it were a relief from serious learning. But for children, play is serious learning. Play is really the work of childhood." – Fred Rogers, *Mr. Rogers Neighborhood*

- *Create your future from your future, not your past. "* – Werner Erhard

- "What is the definition of insanity...doing the same thing over and over again, expecting different results." - Benjamin Franklin

TheAbundanceCenter.com

About The Author: Laurie LaMantia

Laurie LaMantia is an entrepreneurship professor at DePaul University in Chicago, teaching students the processes of creating powerful new businesses that will be a vehicle of prosperity and joy to them and all they interact with.

- She has been studying creating technologies for the last 21 years while immersed in the fields of creativity and innovation.
- She was the co-founder of the Innovation center, IdeaVerse, an award-winning intrepreneurial venture at Lucent Technologies nurturing an environment for creativity and innovation. She also worked in the new ventures organization within AT&T launching new ventures.
- She is the co-author of Breakthrough Teams for Breakneck Times, a guide for unlocking the genius of collaboration.
- She is also the author of Effortless Wealth, a guide for developing your wealth consciousness.
- Laurie hosted her own internet radio show, Making Peace With Money, where she explored the power of prosperity thinking for business and personal affluence.
- **Laurie holds an MBA from Northwestern's Kellogg Graduate School of Management, a Masters in Industrial and Operations Engineering from the University of Michigan and a Bachelor in Electronic Engineering from DeVry University.**
- She is the Chief Prosperity Officer for TheAbundanceCenter.com, a resource filled business dedicated to unlocking the prosperity within each person, every team, and all businesses.
- Laurie is also the sales and marketing director of Reliance Specialty Products, her family's company.
- She is also an artist and owner of Bedazzled Studios, where she creates one-of-a-kind prosperity tables.

Laurie LaMantia

Awareness

Of Your Past

Alchemize

Your Agreements

Awaken

Your Power

Align

Your Energy

Attract

Your Dream

Allow

Your Desires

Amaze

Yourself

©Laurie LaMantia

www.ingramcontent.com/pod-product-compliance
Lightning Source LLC
Chambersburg PA
CBHW050715100426
42735CB00041B/3308